Things I Wish my Mother had Said... (or maybe she did)

Written and Illustrated by

Genie Lee Perron

Balboa Press books may be ordered through booksellers or by contacting:

Balboa Press
A Division of Hay House
1663 Liberty Drive
Bloomington, IN 47403
www.balboapress.com
1-(877) 407-4847

Because of the dynamic nature of the Internet, any web addresses or links contained in this book may have changed since publication and may no longer be valid. The views expressed in this work are solely those of the author and do not necessarily reflect the views of the publisher, and the publisher hereby disclaims any responsibility for them.

ISBN: 978-1-4525-7367-0 (sc)
ISBN: 978-1-4525-7368-7 (e)

Library of Congress Control Number: 2013907901

Printed in the United States of America.

Balboa Press rev. date: 5/7/2013

BALBOA
PRESS
A DIVISION OF HAY HOUSE

This book is dedicated to my mother, Ilene. She was my first teacher, my role model, my hero and my friend. Thank you for your gentle guidance and tremendous wisdom. I was so lucky to have had you as my parent. I love you forever.

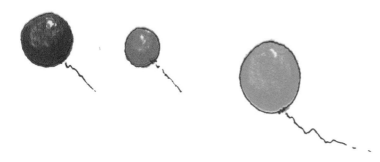

Introduction

Why am I writing this book? I've asked myself this question a million times. After all, the thoughts contained here are not necessarily unique. They have swirled around humanity since the beginning of time. Ancient prophets and modern day teachers have penned variations of these thoughts long before I have. So, my reason for writing this book requires a little back story.

I had the good fortune of being born into a wonderful family. We were your average family, I suppose, with mother, father and three kids. However, I do believe my mother was exceptional. My mom and dad made a good team. Dad was the workaholic, providing for his family and mom the nurturing caregiver.

Mom was very good at her job. We all knew we were loved and although we each had different perspectives and opinions of our parents, we all had our own unique relationships with them. I was the baby of the group and so, by the time I came along, my parents had mellowed a bit and dad worked a bit less. They had a lot more time to spend with me in my growing up and adolescent years.

My mother was ahead of her time. Perhaps being an Army brat and living in so many different places made her a tad more worldly and knowing than your average housewife. She was well-read, very spiritual, and open-minded. As a child, I loved talking with her. I grew up surrounded by books of all kinds. The ones that captured my attention were the various philosophical and spiritual books. We had The Wisdom of Lao Tzu, The Story of Siddhartha, The Prophet, the Bible and on and on kicking around my house. I was fascinated by the various myths, legends and differing outlooks on life.

As I grew to adulthood, my mother became less a parent and more a friend. We had some wonderful discussions and debates. I never felt like she was speaking down to me. She was my best girlfriend. Sure, I had peers that I felt close to, but I always made time for my mom. I loved our chats, our mall walks and I just drank in her wisdom.

When I got married, I knew I wanted to be a mom. I prayed I would be as good a mother as mine. I also hoped I would have the benefit of my mother's gentle guidance to draw upon when I raised my children.

Mom was diagnosed with cancer in the late eighties. Shortly after, I was married. I suffered two miscarriages within a year. I wanted to be pregnant so badly so that my children would know and remember my dear mother. The thought of losing my mother was my biggest fear and sadness at that time. I feared that my mother would pass away and I would not be able to impart the words of wisdom to my offspring that I was so lucky to have had.

I was finally blessed with two beautiful daughters. However, the fear and hopelessness regarding my mother's illness encompassed my every thought and by the year 2000, I had manifested a diagnosis of my own. I was diagnosed with chronic myelogenous leukemia in February of 2000. Four months later, my beloved mother and best friend died. At the time, my daughters were three and four years old.

In the beginning, my prognosis was not good. Treatments available did nothing to reverse my condition, but merely bought time by slowing the progression of disease. I knew I needed to go within to help with my healing. I did lots of meditating, Reiki and other forms of holistic healing in addition to conventional medicine. I was fortunate to start a new, "miracle" drug as it was fast tracked through the FDA. With the help of this drug and through the other holistic methods of healing, I was able to maintain my health and went into remission not long after beginning treatment. I have been in remission for 12 years now.

Along my path to physical healing, I realized that I needed to heal spiritually in order to heal physically. The beautiful side effect to all my meditation and inner work over the years is the discovery that I can still access my mother's wisdom. When I calm myself through meditation or yoga, I can feel my mother's presence as I interact with my children. When I paint or draw, she is right there with me, sharing her joy and artistic talent. I have felt her words flow through me and I know she is rejoicing as she watches, from spirit, the beautiful young women I am raising.

And so, this book, a compilation of original artwork and thoughts, is a tribute to my mother, to her words of wisdom, her kindness, her gentle ways and her pure love of her family. My hope is that this book will somehow preserve my interpretation of her wisdom and that of all the great teachers before her for my children. The most important lesson I learned from my mother is that life is good. It's not always fair and sometimes there are bumps in the road, but it IS good!!!

2

"How wonderful it is that nobody need wait a single moment before starting to improve the world."
-- Anne Frank

Peace

I was an odd child, I think. I remember sitting with my mother as a small child and really worrying about the state of the world. I wondered how people could be so mean to other people just because they might be a different religion or race. I can remember telling her how senseless I thought this was and asking her what could I do to make the world a more peaceful place. I felt so small and insignificant in the grand scheme of things. I believe my mother sensed my almost unnatural worry about such things.

Her words to me were simple. She told me that we can't change the world, but what we can do is make our little section of the world a better place. We can start with ourselves. We can choose to be kinder and gentler in the way we treat ourselves. Then, we can branch out to our immediate family and practice patience and understanding with them. We can really make an effort to see the good in other people. After-all, we are all connected and though the details of another person's life may be different from our own, we all have the same basic wants and needs.

It made me think. How could we achieve a world where people appreciated themselves and also the diversity around them? What steps could we take to make our little piece of Earth more peaceful, joyous and loving? I came to truly understand that in order to change the world, we needed to change our own attitudes and perceptions. We needed as Ghandi said, to "become the change you wish to see in the world".

If we want to see more loving behavior and kindness in the world, we need to be more loving and kind to ourselves and those around us. When we create even small changes in ourselves, those positive changes radiate out into the world like concentric circles. Our new insights and behaviors can bring new light to those around us and ultimately change our world for the better.

Throughout time, people have looked for happiness, peace and even God, somewhere outside themselves. Many don't realize that all happiness, peace, power and indeed God reside right within all of us. In fact, I believe it is our purpose in life to journey through our days learning, growing and seeking joy. In doing so, we can come to the realization that this is the essence of peace.

"A man is but a product of his thoughts.
What he thinks, he becomes."
-- Ghandi

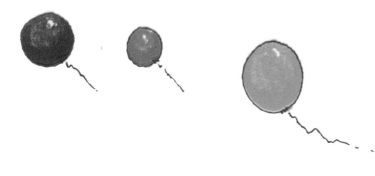

Loving One's Self

So many times, growing up, I would criticize myself. I was either too short or too fat or too loud. The list could go on and on depending on what day of the week or my current mood. Although my mother, thinking she was helping, would certainly mention if she thought I was gaining some pounds, she was also my biggest cheerleader. If she would overhear me criticizing something about myself or calling myself a derogatory name, she would tell me to stop all those negative comments about myself. She said there are far too many insecure people out there that are willing to agree with anyone else's negative views about themselves.

Though mom was not super religious, she was very spiritual and had a firm belief that there was a God. God wasn't some man in a throne judging us all, but my mother used to explain God to me as an energy, like electricity. She used to say that although you can't see electricity, you know it is there because you can observe its effects. And she always stressed that we were all a part of this energy; that our body was our temple here on Earth, the house of our soul. With that in mind, we should do everything in our power to take good care of our bodies and to love them because doing anything less is doing a disservice to your soul, your spark of divinity. We are all perfect reflections of God.

So, as I matured and started to understand more of what my mother was trying to impart to me, I began to realize that if we didn't love ourselves, we could not truly love others. It started to make sense that loving one's self is the first step to peace on Earth. We make peace with ourselves, and then we can find that peace in our own external world. Appreciation of self leads to inner peace which eventually translates to outer peace.

Now, think for a moment about how you talk to yourself. Are the voices in your mind kind to you or do you habitually find fault with yourself and others? Our self-talk can either serve us or not, but one thing is for sure, we get to control it. We are the only ones in our own head! Our thoughts are so powerful and the thrilling thing about this realization is that we are the masters of them!

One of my favorite modern day teachers is Louise Hay. Her affirmations and writings have helped me through many tough times in my life. I think one of the most powerful tools for self-empowerment that she recommends is called mirror work. It is a great, yet simple means for fostering approval, appreciation and acceptance of one's self.

Mirror work is an easy process. Simply find a mirror and look yourself in the eyes and tell yourself, "I love you. I really, really love you." You can continue on with more of your positive aspects if you are so inclined. When you first begin the process, it will probably feel very strange to you. So, my suggestion is to start small. Talk to yourself in the mirror in the morning and evening and keep it as brief as you feel comfortable. Really make a conscious effort to do this every day and give it enough time to make it a habit. As time goes by, I bet you will really come to enjoy your chats with yourself.

What I found amazing as I began this work is the amount of negative chatter about me that I had going on in my brain! I always thought I was such a nice person, so how could I be so mean to me? Think about that.

As you continue your mirror work, simply observe your inner voice without judgment. Don't beat yourself up for any negativity you might notice. Remember, you have the power to shift your thoughts at any moment to those that feel better and are more soothing and beneficial. Over time, being kind and loving to yourself will become easier. As you become more aware, you can catch your not-so-nice thoughts quicker and flip them right over to more positive, loving thoughts.

Soon, believe it or not, you will find the predominance of your thoughts is much more beneficial than when you started. As you continue to practice, you will find positive changes occurring in your life. The wonderfully "magical" thing about this is, you begin to attract from life all the beauty and goodness you deserve!

Love your body. Study nutrition and experiment with healthy foods that taste good and nourish your body. Drink lots of pure water and move your body. It was built for movement. As you consciously show yourself love, your body and soul will thrive.

Surround yourself with positive people. Be available to help them, but also allow them to offer assistance to you too if you need it. Giving and receiving love and support are important acts of self-love.

This work is so important. How does it help to bring about a more peaceful planet for all of us? People that feel good about themselves do not need to try and control others or make others feel badly. In other words, when you are connected to that beautiful force that is God, or the goodness of life, you cannot do harm to another. So, when we truly love ourselves, we can then achieve more constant inner peace. And then, we can create a more peaceful environment around us. This leads full circle to a better more peaceful world for all.

The greatest part of all this work, for me, is that now, when I look into the mirror and tell myself that I really love me, I can see my mother smiling back at me. I think she knows I am starting to get it……

"If the only prayer you said in your whole life was, "thank you," that would suffice."
-- Meister Eckhart

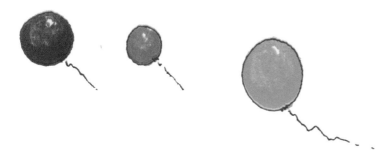

Gratitude

Mom set a good example for all of us. Every morning, she would awaken and open her bedroom shades uniformly. She would stretch and thank God for another beautiful day. She lived her life with a sense of gratitude and grace. She knew that riches didn't mean just financial abundance, but that abundance was all around us in the sunsets and the children laughing and the people we love. After her diagnosis, I believe she became even more aware of the little things in life and how much they meant to her. Even when those close to her knew how she suffered physically from the effects of her illness, she always said (and believed) that she was "doing fine….better every day".

As I began to face my own dis-ease, I realized quite profoundly, that she was onto something big. When I was diagnosed, I knew that despite what the doctors said about my prognosis, only God knew how much time I had left here on Earth. I knew, innately, that if I gave the word leukemia the power, that I would surely live up to the doctor's morbid expectations of me. At that point, I had two preschoolers to get raised. There was no way I was going to leave them.

I had to start focusing on living each day as a thank you. Every moment, we have the opportunity to focus on things that give us pleasure or things that bring pain. When we focus on all the things, big and small, for which we are grateful, we send out a beacon to the Universe that says, "I like this…send more, please!".

Each morning since my diagnosis, I awaken and the first thought in my head as I stretch is, I am healthy and strong. Then, before arising, I make a mental list of everything in my life that I appreciate and for which I am so grateful. Sometimes my list is very general, like being thankful for being alive or being able to sit up, stretch and get out of bed. Other days my list is quite specific, like being thankful I found that great shirt or that I have such fabulous people in my life or had that great meal.

Each night before bed, I write in my gratitude journal. I find at least five things for which I am thankful. Sometimes I simply rattle off a list and sometimes, if I am feeling creative, I write a "brief" essay. This very simple act of being grateful and appreciative brings more wonderful experiences into your life. The more you graciously appreciate all the things in your life that are going right, the more things start to go right for you!

There is so much in life for which to be thankful. Try this process in your own life. It's another simple process with seemingly magical effects. Each night before you go to bed, sit quietly and breathe as you review your day. Then, either in your journal or at least consciously in your mind, make a list of at least five things for which you are grateful. Feel free to list more if you can. Some days it may feel like a struggle, but dig deep and do it. The more you practice observing the positive aspects of your days, the easier it gets. If you find you can rattle off more, keep going. List as many as you can and if you're on a roll, stay with it!

The more you can create an attitude of gratitude in your life, the more you will see your world turn around for the better. As if by magic, things will start to go easier for you. Life will become your friend and together you will create a truly magnificent reality!

Appreciation for life's blessings opens a valve for more and more delicious, delightful splendors. Start now! You will not regret it!

(Thanks, Mom)

"Watch your thoughts, for they become words. Watch your words, for they become actions. Watch your actions, for they become habits. Watch your habits, for they become character. Watch your character, for it becomes your destiny."
–Unknown

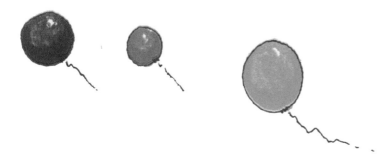

Peace Within

Ahhhh, the sound of bliss and inner peace, we all crave that Ahhhhhh feeling. Finding that place is really as easy as breathing. We just need to learn to quiet our minds and to reconnect with the ever-present stream of well-being. OK…maybe it's not always that simple, but with practice and dedication, we can all get to a more peaceful mindset.

It is our birthright to feel peace and joy. Some of us lose sight of that from time to time as we go through our hectic lives. In today's fast-paced, instant information world, it is easy to feel rushed, disconnected, frustrated and downright stressed. We all need a way to detach from the frenzy of everyday life.

I suggest that meditation is the most powerful tool for turning off your mind and reconnecting with the peace and tranquility of life. Don't let the word meditation scare you. There is no right or wrong method. The key to success is to set aside a small block of time for yourself and to just do it. There are so many methods, CDs, guided meditations and styles out there. I will list some of my favorites in the Resource section at the end of the book. If you can dedicate just fifteen minutes a day for sitting in quiet reflection, over time you will find yourself feeling calmer and more centered. You will learn to quiet the multitude of thoughts in your head.

I have read that each day we think something like 60,000 thoughts. This background noise is something we are all very accustomed to. However, it will go on and on incessantly unless we do something consciously to stop it. Now, obviously there is a need for our thoughts in our everyday life. I maintain that if we dedicate a small amount of time to quiet and regeneration, then the multitude of thoughts in our brains will be more productive. We'll be in a calmer place and will be able to process our thoughts much more effectively.

One of the simplest techniques for quieting the mind is to sit in a quiet space. Breathe in for a count of four and then out for a count of four. Focus on your breath as you breathe in and out easily. Let your breath be smooth and natural. Physiologically, your body will respond positively by slowing your heart rate a bit and relaxing.

If thoughts come up or emotions surface, simply observe them without judgment. You might say to yourself, "thinking", and then direct your thoughts back to your breathing. Remember that there is no right or wrong. It's called the practice of meditation. You don't need to be perfect!

Many find it nice to have a notebook or journal handy for after meditating. Perhaps you can record any thoughts that came up and ask for guidance on those thoughts in your next quiet time. Sometimes people get inspiration for projects they may be working on. You just never know what will come up in a meditation, but it's all good! Remember there is no right or wrong.

Some enjoy quiet music playing in the background. I will list some of my favorites in the Resource section. Others light candles or burn incense. No matter what tools you choose to enhance your practice, it is important that you set aside time and space each day. Make it a habit. Make yourself and your calmness and well-being a priority to you!

Remember to focus on your breathing. Be calm and reserve judgment or criticism. Don't beat yourself up if your mind wanders. Just guide yourself gently back to quiet. As you continue your meditation practice, you will find it easier to quiet your mind. You will quite possibly find you crave your quiet time. Above all just enjoy it!

I think it's important to mention that meditation doesn't always have to be so formal. There are many things we do each day that can bring us to that peace place in our mind. Gazing at the stars, listening to soothing music, drawing or even doing the dishes can be calming in their own right.

My mother was not really into conventional meditation. She knew of meditation, but she found her peace and quiet in other ways. Throughout her life, she found peace while painting or sketching. Some of my fondest childhood memories are of mom teaching me how to draw a body in proportion or the anatomy of a face. I loved watching her work and trying to perfect my own techniques. To this day, I feel her with me when I am absorbed in drawing or creating.

Later in her life, as she was dealing with her illness, she would distract herself by drawing adorable, happy, little clowns which she called, "Redheads by Ilene". She and my dad would travel to craft fairs and sell her framed or matted works. It gave her great joy to create her unique artwork and to share it with the world. On the dedication page of this book is just one of many of her beloved Redheads.

As I grew, I became very interested in traditional meditation and other healing techniques. I studied Reiki, went to drumming circles, attended meditation groups and continue to be drawn to that type of peaceful quiet time to this day. I actually introduced my mother to some of the techniques. One instance pops into mind vividly. It was around my mom's birthday and I decided to take her to a meditation group in a nearby town at a healing center there. I thought it would be cool to invite my sister along as well. The three of us arrived at this regal Victorian home on the water. Naturally, we entered the room with the proper amount of seriousness and decorum.

Well, the group consisted of about eight females and one male. The lovely, soft-spoken leader of the meditation began by telling us to breathe. While breathing, we were to envision a beautiful, white light traveling from our feet all the way to our heads and out of our crown chakra. I don't know how long the meditation lasted, but afterwards, the leader asked if anyone wanted to share their impressions. The lone male in the group raised his hand and proceeded to say, "I can see the white light, but I can't get it up."

I *can* be mature, but when you pair me with my sister and somebody says THAT. I thought initially, I shouldn't look at my sister. Sadly, I didn't follow my own advice. I glanced at her and she looked back at me. We both tried stifling our laughter. This made it even worse because the "muffled" sound that emanated from our mouths was horrendous. As all heads turned to stare, my mother sat on the other end of the couch pretending she didn't know us. Needless to say, she never went back to a meditation group with me and my sister.

Moral of the story, have fun! Don't be afraid to explore the many techniques that are available to quiet your mind. Make yourself a priority. If you don't make time for you, who will? Start small, just five minutes a day if that's all the time you can muster at first, but please do make it a part of your daily ritual. I know you won't regret it!

"Darkness cannot drive out darkness; only light can do that."
– Dr. Martin Luther King, Jr

Look for the Positive

*I*n any situation, there are positive aspects and some not-so positive. Our goal, as we work towards attaining a greater level of inner peace, is to train our focus, what we think about, toward the positive side as much as possible. We really do get to decide where we place our attention.

There will always be challenges in life. We are here to learn and grow. Most of us learn by trying new things perhaps succeeding on our first try or perhaps stumbling a bit. If things always went smoothly, how would we learn at all? We learn and grow by living our lives, making mistakes, gaining whatever wisdom we can from those mistakes and then picking ourselves up and carrying on.

Abraham-Hicks, another of my favorite modern day teachers, talks about every subject consisting of wanted and unwanted elements. Our individual power comes from the fact that we get to decide on which part to focus. Do you realize how powerful that is?

Let's take a concrete example. Suppose you have just broken up with a romantic partner. Of course you will go through a period of sadness. However, you now stand at a crossroad. You can choose to focus on the negative side; I'm alone, my heart is broken, I will never find another love, He/she was perfect for me and there's nobody else out there that will get me, etc. My mother used to call this wallowing in self-pity. Or, you can shift your perspective and focus on the more positive side. For instance; now I have more freedom, I can get to know myself more and develop unexplored talents, I can pursue my own interests, I don't have to check in with anyone about my plans, I can work to better myself and be a better me.

In the example above, the actual situation or life experience didn't change at all. However, we changed our way of looking at it. Just typing the positive outlook shifted my energy. Imagine if you could get in the habit or automatically changing the way you looked at things. Wayne Dyer, another favorite teacher of mine, has a saying, "when you change the way you look at things, the things you look at change." It is so true and that, like many other life skills, becomes easier the more you practice it in your actual life.

Events in our lives are only good or bad because of our perceptions of them. Take my diagnosis of leukemia for example. At age 35, with two small children, this could be looked at as a major tragedy. Perhaps, at first, I did think of it as the worst thing ever. Overtime though, I have come to see my diagnosis as a blessing.

Too many positive changes came about in my life because of it to see it any other way. I was able to stay home with my children. I saw, firsthand, the amazing healing capabilities of the body when the mind is focused as positively as possible. I witnessed the mind/body connection and saw how powerful that is. I made myself and my well-being a priority, since I realized that if I didn't take care of myself, I would be of no use to those I loved. I developed an appreciation of the simple things in life. Every day became a gift. I started learning how to live in the moment, since that moment in time is all we have. I could go on and on.

By training yourself to look at the brighter side of any situation, you can shift the focus and quality of your life. Now, as you get better at this, you will find that it becomes automatic. You will be faced with challenges and contrasts throughout your life and you will instinctively focus on the brighter aspect of each situation. You will find it easier to make peace with exactly where you are.

"Nothing ever happened in the past that can prevent you from being present now; and if the past cannot prevent you from being present now, what power does it have?"
–Eckhart Tolle

The Past is the Past
Or
Live in the Now

My mother always told me to live each day. Don't fuss about the past because what's done is done. Each moment that you live, you are propelling yourself into your present. The present is where life is lived.

Live your life in the present moment as much as you can. It's great to have dreams for your future. In fact, I think it's necessary to have big dreams. That's how we motivate ourselves to move towards those things and experiences in life that we want. However, don't get so fixated on the specific details of your dream. Life sees the big picture, to which we are not always privy. As we grow and mature, hopefully, we begin to see that life always puts us right where we're meant to be. We are bringing experiences to us that match the things our soul needs in order to grow.

Is life always going to be easy or perfect? Nope, but remembering that I am always where I am meant to be has given me a sense of peace. Anything life sends me, I know I have the capacity to handle because if I didn't, I wouldn't be experiencing it at all. We are always stronger than we think we are!

If we can just know in our hearts that every moment we are doing the best we can, then there is nothing more anyone can ask of us. So, if in each moment we are doing our very best, then even mistakes we have made along the way are OK. They may have served to guide us to better actions in the future. Perhaps they have taught us something about ourselves. But, no matter what, it's all good because we honestly know we have done our best.

We can carry that even further by saying that if I'm always doing my best, then I suppose others are doing the best they can with their knowledge at any given time. We can then, perhaps, stop judging and criticizing other's choices. We can cut other people a bit of slack for things we possibly find offensive or displeasing.

There is truly no point in mulling over or trying to dissect your past. You might never get it all figured out, for life is fluid and ever-changing and we are always growing and learning. Your time would be better spent on living in your Now, where you can actually live and make corrections. Be open and observe memories from the past. Honor them and enjoy them if they are fond memories, but you do not have to let the less pleasing ones trouble you.

You don't need to go back and fix anything from your past. What's done is done. Furthermore, you already carry the vibes of unresolved issues from your past into your present. Your present moment is the only place where life is being lived. So, at any moment you can decide to look at things differently and to make changes in your outlook and/or opinions. You never have to make reparations for things in the past. Simply resolve to do better and make better choices in your now.

Your past brought you to your present and made you the wonderful person you are today. You should LOVE who you are. You need not be perfect, but ponder this. You are perfect BECAUSE of your imperfections. It is through your mistakes that you learn and grow and that is what life is all about.

So, ride the wave. Life is full of ups and downs. Without the down times, how could we begin to appreciate the ups? When you're feeling low realize that you are on the cusp of growth. Life is showing you things that you may not particularly care to see, but if you can make the conscious effort to say to yourself, "hey, I don't like this or that...what is it I would like?" Then you can little by little shift your focus to the things you DO want. As you practice controlling the only real thing you can control....your thoughts, then you will begin to see your life change in seemingly remarkable ways. This is our true power...it's within each and every one of us.

" I have decided to be happy because it is good for my health."
-- Voltaire

Things That Bring You Joy

OK, so we have learned that we get to control our thoughts and that they are very powerful creative forces. Here is what I think is the next most important step. Finding things that bring you joy.

Ultimately, the purpose of life is joy. What better way to bring happiness into your life than to focus on those things that bring you joy? Life is so full of simple pleasures.

Each of us will have our own set of pleasures. For some, seeing a beautiful sunset brings joy. For others, a concert of classical music makes you smile. And others may really get turned on by a big hunk of chocolate cake. Personally, I'll take all of the above!

My mother was always one to point out the small treasures and wonders in the world around us. We spent one whole spring and summer when I was a child watching a family of cardinals lay their eggs, raise their young and then finally bid their young brood adieu. It was beautiful and I still hold that memory so dear. I can't tell you how many gorgeous sunsets my mother would "force" us to stop and look at so we didn't miss the beauty of nature all around us. Looking back, I see how lucky I was to have such an appreciation instilled upon me from the very beginning of my life.

Anyway, the important thing to remember is no matter what it is that brings you joy, practice noticing and appreciating those things. The more you place your attention on these pleasurable things, the more Life works to bring you more. Feelings are your guidance system. They show you where your focus lies and what your point of attraction is. Practice looking for things that bring you a feeling of contentment.

Use your emotions and feelings as guideposts. Train your thoughts so that you can easily evoke a sense of contentment in your life. This is easy to do if you set aside some quiet time each day for yourself. When you have none of the distractions of daily life, you can more easily concentrate on finding those blissful thoughts and feelings. Then, the key (and the big test) is to make the conscious effort to maintain that sense of balance when you are faced with circumstances out in the real world. You know you've acquired some good focusing skills when you can be in the midst of chaos and still feel truly calm on the inside.

Sometimes people around you will be having a rough time. It can be easy to get swept into their chaos. Please don't do it. Stay calm. Now, this doesn't mean that you don't care about others or what might be going on in their lives. Quite the opposite, it means you do care, deeply. You care so much, in fact, that you know if you get swept up in their problems, you are of no use to them anyway. Only by remaining calm and connected to your own source of power can you help anyone else. So, you feel compassion for people you observe that may be going through rough times, but you do not get swept away by the negative emotions they might be feeling. You can be like a lighthouse is to a boat on the ocean in a raging storm. You shine your light and as they calmly seek solutions, they can be guided to safety by that light.

Life is really about the journey. The end result is actually just a starting point for more experiences and desires. As you achieve more of your goals, your wants grow and so do your dreams. That is the stuff of life; growth, achieving desires and growing towards new expanded wishes. So, if you can enjoy the process of getting from point A to point B, you will soon find that your desires, both big and small, flow to you effortlessly.

Make joy the key. Find joy in the simple things. Laugh more than you cry. Think about, dream about and talk about all the juicy, wonderful, phenomenal, earth shaking, toe curling, howling things that bring you joy!

SMILE….Life is so good!

" Nothing external has any power over me."
– Walt Whitman

Hate Destroys the Vessel in Which It's Stored and Not the One on Which It's Poured

I don't know where my mother picked up this quote, but it is one that I heard quite frequently growing up. As a child, I can remember hearing this when I would complain about some person or event in my life. I am sure there were times when I even ranted about hating someone or something. Each and every time, there was Mom with this handy dandy phrase, "Hate destroys the vessel in which it's stored and not the one on which it's poured". As with many of Mom's sayings, it took a while to settle in.

Think about it. When you spend time wallowing in the negative energy of hatred, how is your body feeling? My experience is that I just feel crappier and grumpier the more I focus on all those bad vibes. Meanwhile, the object of my extreme dislike, anger and hostility is blissfully unaware of me stewing. I am not affecting anything positively. Instead, I am allowing myself to stay in a negative emotional state.

To me, it feels like I am giving away my power. I am wasting my own time, instead of enjoying the beauty around me. The older I get, the more I realize that life is too short to spend a lot of time hating.

It all keeps pointing back to the fact that we all control only one thing, our thoughts. We can choose at any moment to shift from hatred, fear or anger to love, peace and joy. It takes practice to pivot your thoughts, but the more you train them toward positivity, the easier it gets. Don't let hatred destroy your vessel. You DO get to control that!

"When you change the way you look at things,
the things you look at change"
-- Wayne Dyer

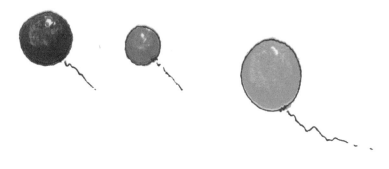

Diversity

There is more than one path to peace, joy, and divinity. Each of us enters this world as the perfect reflection of love and life. We are part of that same universal energy called God or Source or the Creator. We all have different viewpoints and perceptions. We have different likes and dislikes.

This is the beauty of life. If we were all the same, with identical passions and aversions, life would be incredibly dull. It would be much like a quilt with one color or a monochromatic uniformly textured painting. In a word, life would be boring.

If we can learn to embrace the diversity in life and in each other, we gain a tremendous amount of personal freedom. We no longer need to convince others that only our point of view is correct. We do not have to defend our perspective. We can simply live and let live. No longer would we waste time and energy fearing and fighting about those things we don't understand.

Don't beat up on yourself when you get annoyed at certain behaviors you see in other people. You are in the process of growing, so when you notice things occurring in your environment that you might find displeasing or offensive, it can pull you back into an old thought pattern. It bothers you more because now you are more aware. You care more about where you direct your thoughts and about how you feel. It's all normal and I would take it as a good sign. You are growing and changing. Your ways of looking at the world and your own behaviors and coping mechanisms are constantly being revamped. It's good. It's really good.

So, try to continue to practice observing without judgment. Just appreciate that what you are noticing may not be how you would handle a particular situation, but it is OK. Whoever you are watching or whatever circumstance has gotten your attention is happening for them and they are dealing with it in the best way they can.

As you lighten up on yourself and others, life becomes a joy. We can all peacefully follow our own paths. We joyously dance through life to our own music. We are not hurting anyone and so we simply enjoy our life experiences while pursuing that which brings us joy.

Try to open your heart and mind to new ideas and perspectives. Be amazed at the uniqueness of all the beings here on Earth. You may not understand or even agree with what you see, but that isn't important in the grand scheme of things. Be an individual. Be yourself and as you go peacefully about your day doing things that you enjoy, allow others that same luxury.

What a wonderful place this is. To know that it is safe for me to be me and also for you to be you. We can live in harmony with one another. That is peace within and without.

"When one door of happiness closes, another opens; but often we look so long at the closed door that we do not see the one that has been opened for us."
-- Helen Keller

The Ups and Downs of Life

In every life there will be times of peace and there will be times when things around us feel out of control and not so positive. This is normal. It is how life is supposed to be. The adversities we face and overcome serve to strengthen us. Our triumphs, even in the face of what seems like catastrophe, tempers us.

You do not have to paste a smile on your face when things really suck. However, you will benefit greatly if you can nip the negative in the bud. If what you are observing in your life is making you fussy, your mission is to try and stop the momentum of the negative thoughts. You see, negative thoughts love company and so the more you think them, the more friends of the negative variety they invite along to join you. Before you know it, you could have quite the negativity free-for-all going on!

Realize that where you are and what you are experiencing serves the purpose of clarifying what you do want. So, as quickly as you can, take some nice deep breaths, calm yourself and recognize that things always work out for you. Remember that somehow you always land on your feet and that you are a survivor. Remind yourself that no matter how terrible something may seem at the time, when you look back on the event later, it never seems that bad. You got through it! Not only did you survive, but you're thriving.

The way you look at the situations in your life dictates the tone for your experiences. You are the one in control of your own perceptions and thoughts. Don't worry about the things you can't control. You can't control other people, the way they think, or your environment. However, you can control your thoughts and your reaction to your surroundings. Please do not give away your power by allowing outside influences to control your thoughts and feelings.

"Imagination is everything. It is the preview of life's coming attractions."
– Albert Einstein

Tell Your Story the Way You Want it to Be

*M*any people go through their lives observing situations, circumstances and events and telling narratives about these events to everyone they meet. Now, if the situation is a pleasing one, it is very beneficial to tell the story repeatedly. It makes you feel good to remember the pleasant details.

However, if the circumstances in your life are not exactly ideal or even painful, you really do not want to rehash them over and over thereby giving more energy to them. There is a way to live your life and make subtle changes in the way you tell your story.

I want to share a very powerful and effective tool for redirecting your life. I have used this tool regularly for many years and I am amazed at how effective it is. The tool is called Intention Writing.

Intention Writing, or as some call it, Scripting, is a process by which you write a description of things in your life, but you write it in such a way as you are telling the story as you want it to be. Your writing may not be exactly how things are presently, but it reflects things the way you want them to be.

To begin, buy yourself an attractive journal or notebook, one that makes you happy just to look at it. Think about a facet of your life, perhaps your current job or a relationship. Now take a moment to envision this subject the way you want it to be, your ideal version. As you write, tell your story in the present tense. Say things like, "I have the perfect job. The requirements of the position I hold suit my abilities and strengths perfectly. I love going to work. I have the most amazing and enjoyable people around me". Continue writing the most positive version of your story that you can. Always write in present tense because you want to really feel like what you desire is already happening.

During a particular time in my life, I wrote every night in my pretty journal about a situation that I wanted to change. I wrote from my heart about the way I truly wanted this to be. Each night, I would read what I had written before and smile as I read. Over time, it seemed so natural that what I was reading really was true.

It is interesting to me that most of what I have written about in the past has come to fruition in my life. This tool helps you to focus your thoughts. As we already know, our thoughts create our reality and if we can focus them towards the positive, we can create quite the nice little life for ourselves.

You are painting the picture of your life. You have all the tools you need to create a joyous, colorful masterpiece. A painting, like life, has more depth and meaning because of the light and shadows it contains. You hold the brush. You paint the picture.

Everything you view as reality right now, started as a dream or a thought. You are living the creations you brought forth from previous visualizations and wants. In this present moment, your Now, if you can continue to tell the story of your life as you want it to be, you will be creating from this new and improved place. Because you are deliberately seeking more joy in the present moment, you are painting your picture on a better canvas with better quality paints.

Conclusion

J am in awe of the full circle my life has taken. Having the benefit of growing up in the family that I did helped to lay a solid foundation for me. As a child, I listened to my mother's words, sometimes annoyed by the "wisdom" she was trying to impart. As a mother, I see with new eyes, from a different perspective.

I know that my children roll their eyes as I tell them the same things over and over. However, I also know that they are taking in the words and thoughts that resonate with them and making their own personal philosophies. They will change and build on my ideas to suit their wonderful expanding lives. My children will find their way through life's ups and downs just as I did and as generations before me did and after me will.

I've learned that although those we love may leave us in the physical realm, they are never more than a thought or memory away. And, if we can quiet the hum of our thoughts long enough, we can possibly still hear their profound and loving words. As we pursue things that give us joy, they are right there with us, cheering us on or picking us up when we fall. That love never, ever goes away.

So, no matter what your upbringing was, just know that you have all the tools you need to turn your life into exactly what you want it to be. The power of your thoughts is yours to control. Some people may have lots of turmoil and struggle early in their lives, while others may have an easy childhood, but face more challenges later in life. No matter which is true for you, remember that whatever you experience in life is helping you to grow. If it doesn't kill you, it does make you stronger and although it may not feel like it at the time, each little challenge that you face and conquer is a blessing.

You are in the driver's seat. Life is good and it is what you make it. You get to steer the wheel!!!

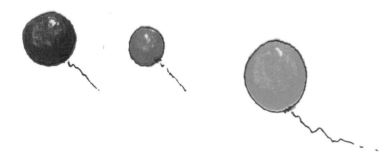

Many Thanks

There are so many people I want to thank for making this book and my outlook on life possible. First, my parents, you were my very first teachers. You taught me to respect others, to value life, to treat people the way I want to be treated and to love myself. I miss you both, but I feel your presence from spirit more and more. I love you.

To my brother and sister; we grew up together. I learned so much by watching you both. Though we may not see each other often, we shared the best parents on Earth and I am lucky to have you in my life. Thanks for being a part of my family.

To my beautiful family; Scott, my love and my two beautiful daughters, Deanna and Debbie, there are no words to express how deeply I love you. You make each day worth living. I am so privileged to have you all in my life. Thanks for helping me learn, love and grow.

To my friends both old and new, you've been there to listen and offer reassurance when things were rough. And, you've celebrated with me when things went well. You are all reflections of different aspects of my personality and I appreciate each of you more than words can tell. I am so lucky to be surrounded by such positive, wonderful human beings.

To the many teachers I have met along the way, thank you. There have been so many authors and speakers that have influenced me in positive ways. You have helped reinforce the words I heard from childhood. You've helped me to practice those teachings to enrich my life.

And, finally, thank you to the wonderful people at Balboa Press. You helped make this work a joy. Your expertise and encouragement was invaluable.

Resources

Books

Hicks, Esther and Jerry. "Ask and it is Given". Carlsbad, CA: Hay House, 2004.

Hay, Louise L. "You Can Heal Your Life". Carlsbad, CA: Hay House, 1999.

Ban Breathnach, Sarah. "Simple Abundance, A Daybook of Comfort and Joy". New York: Warner Books, 1995.

Ruiz, Don Miguel. "The Four Agreements, a Toltec Wisdom Book". San Rafael, CA: Amber Allen Publishing, 1997.

Tolle, Eckhart. "A New Earth, Awakening to Your Life's Purpose". New York: Penguin Group, 2005.

Dyer, Dr. Wayne W. "Change Your Thoughts-Change Your Life, Living the Wisdom of the Tao". Carlsbad, CA: Hay House, 2007.

Zukav, Gary. "The Seat of the Soul". New York: Simon and Schuster, 1989.

Hay, Louise and Richardson Cheryl. "You Can Create an Exceptional Life". Carlsbad, CA: Hay House, 2011.

Meditation CDs

Kempton, Sally.(2001). Beginning Meditation. [Audio CD]. Sounds True.

Dyer, Wayne. (2012). I am Wishes Fulfilled Meditation. [Audio CD]. Hay House Audio.

Hicks, Esther and Jerry. (2010). Getting Into the Vortex. Guided Meditation and User Guide. [Audio CD]. Hay House.

Eisenberg, Mattie. (2012). Guided Meditations. [Audio CD]. Eisenberg Recordings.

Music

Tolle, Eckhart. (2008). Music to Quiet the Mind. [Audio CD]. Sounds True.

Jarry, Francine. (2007). A New Adventure. [Audio CD]. Jarry Recording.

CPSIA information can be obtained
at www.ICGtesting.com
Printed in the USA
LVIC01n0453190913
352977LV00001BA

9 781452 573670